1 2 3, MOVE WITH ME!

A Creative Movement Adventure

Story and Illustrations
by Kerry Allan

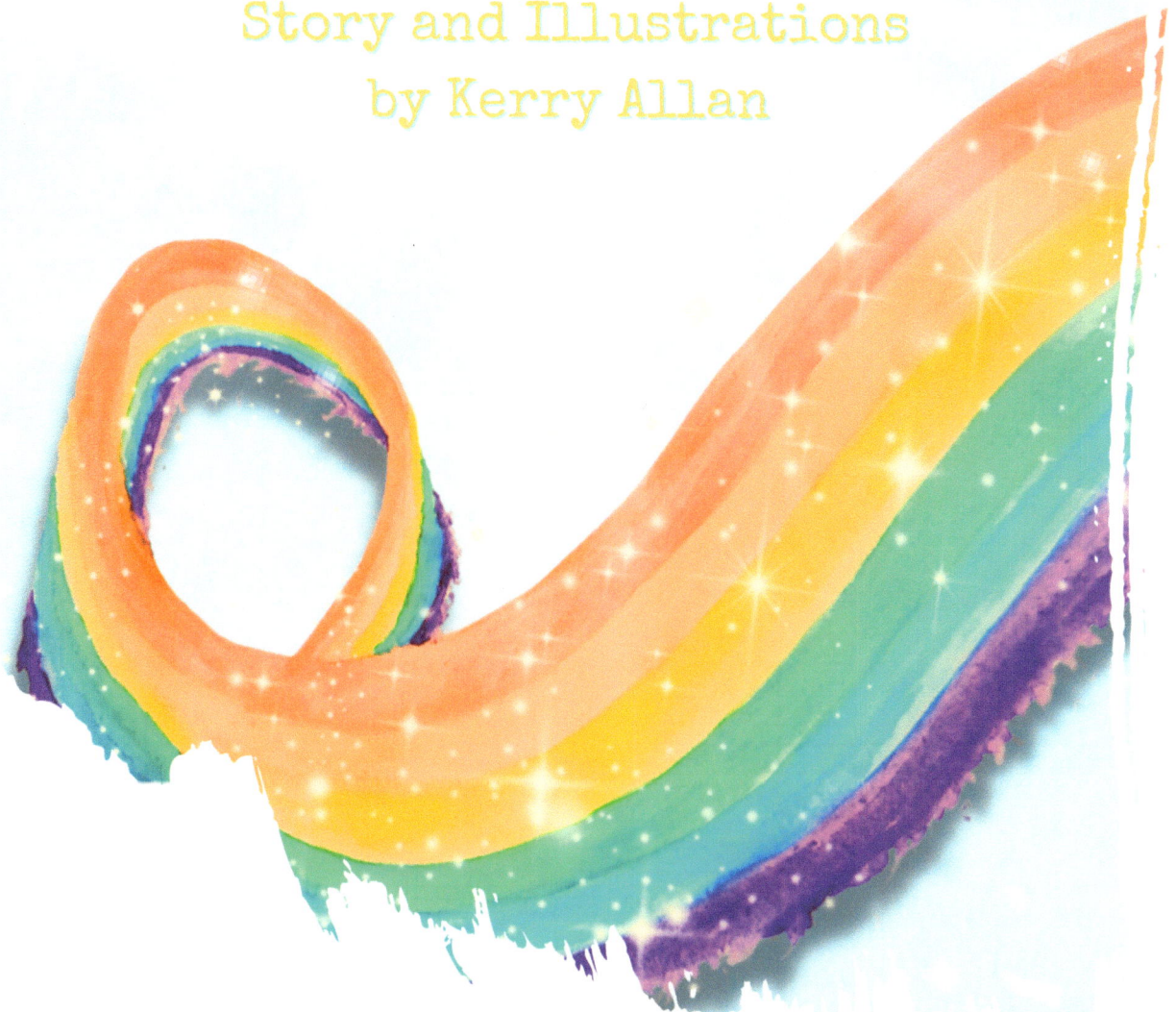

To my first one-of-a-kind young mover, A, and my
newest addition, C, who has enthusiastically
frolicked for my camera in order to lend images to
this book.

Special thanks to my first readers and editors.

--K.A.

1 2 3, MOVE WITH ME!
A Creative Movement Adventure

Story and Illustrations by Kerry Allan

ISBN: 979-8-218-54401-0
Library of Congress: 2024921066

E. Gads Hill Press
TWINKLINGS
for young readers

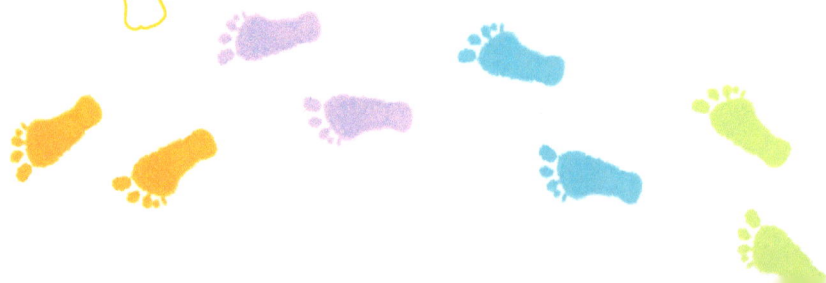

Every day, Emily loves to

MOVE!

When she wakes and hears
the bright birds
start to tweet,

Her body tells her
she has got to
move her feet!

Wiggle,
squiggle,
stretch,
and reach up
to the sun,

Twirling whirling
shapes; moving is
so much fun.

1 2 3, MOVE WITH ME!

FLUTTERING

BUTTERFLY STRETCH

DELICATE

GENTLE

LIGHT

Starting on the ground with feet pressed
oh so tight,

Her open knees become wings and take
off in flight.

Swirling through a meadow with a thousand friends,
Flitter-fluttering until the sunshine ends,

ROOT TO RISE

To the yard and squeezed in like a
seed, so small,

Emily begins to grow
until she's...

1 2 3, MOVE WITH ME!

Fig 1

Fig. 2

TALL

Fig. 3

STRONG GROWING STRETCHED STABLE

Her feet the roots,

her arms the branches

of a tree,

Green finger leaves

will sway as summer

winds blow free.

Now on to class, she stands
with feet placed like a 'V'

And sees a shape that fills the
slot with sides of three:

A TRIANGLE!

It fits between
her toes, how nice...

1 2 3,
MOVE
WITH
ME!

STEADY   PRESSED

OPEN   GRACEFUL

1st POSITION

But better yet if
it becomes a
pizza slice!

Oooh, yum!!

CENTERED LIFTED BALANCED DARING

1 2 3, MOVE WITH ME!

PASSÉ BALANCE

She falls and giggles!

It was worth a try.

She joins flamingos
balancing all
in a row,

1, 2, 3, 4 -- Oh!
Her pink bird
roams below.

1 2 3, MOVE WITH ME!

FREE

JOYFUL

LEAP

Now, finally, a chance to feel her

body SOAR.

Big running leaps are streaking her

across the floor!

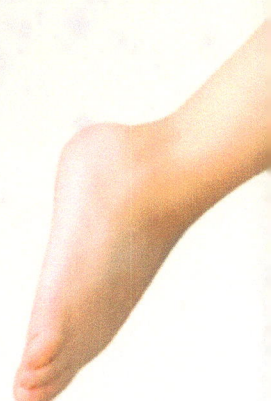

EXCITING FLYING

She lifts into the air,
twirling and floating high
With dazzling creatures flung
across a sunset sky.

1 2 3, MOVE WITH ME!

POWERFUL   HUGE   FIERCE   BRAVE

STOMP

When class is over
Emily is moving still:

Giant **BOOMS** from
thunder shoes crack
down with will.

1 2 3, MOVE WITH ME!

But Mommy says we

TIPTOE

need to hurry to the car. So, we trot

like nimble foxes with swift

SNEAKY

QUICK

PADDED

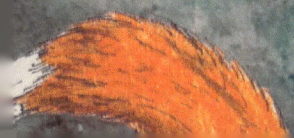

Emily keeps moving with no end in sight;

She's moved and she is moving
well into the night.

And as the stars shine and she's
warmly tucked in bed,

Her universe of dancing dreams
will fill her head.

THE END

WANT TO GET MOVING? DANCE ALONG WITH EMILY!

BUTTERFLY STRETCH

Sit on the floor with your feet pressed together, knees out wide, and back stretched tall! Ready to fly, little butterflies? Okay! Wiggle your knees SLOW in tiny beats of your butterfly wings to fly high. What color is your butterfly? Now, beat your wings small and QUICK to get to that wildflower field! Ahhhh, you've landed on a beautiful flower. Let's dip our noses down to its petals to take a sniff. Lovely! Do your hips feel stretched?

ROOT TO RISE

Calling all seeds to plant a tree! Curl up your body SMALL and low to plant your seed, then give it a little water and light to start growing BIG, bigger, and even bigger. Now your tall tree has strong feet roots and wide arm branches. Can you feel the wind tickle your finger leaves, too? Ooh, it's getting windier! Have fun rocking your branches gently, then wildly, in the breeze!

1st POSITION

Did you know there are 5 positions of the feet in BALLET? Our first position should connect your heels with your toes far enough apart that you could fit a delicious pizza slice in between them! Try bending your knees in first position -- that's called a PLIÉ! Now, see if you can lean over from your waist to take an imaginary bite out of your pizza. Don't lose your first position, though! Can you lift up to stand tall again?

Check out the other positions of the feet:

1st:	2nd:	3rd:	4th:	5th:

PASSÉ BALANCE

Passé like a flamingo by lifting one knee up, with your pointed toes touching the inside of your standing leg! Sound hard? It is! You can start by holding on to a steady object or grown-up. Then, see if you can do it all on your own, feeling your center squeeze to BALANCE like a champ, for 1, 2, 3, 4 counts! Try the other leg, too. Lifting your knee to the front is a parallel balance, used in JAZZ or MODERN dance, but you can also try lifting your knee to the side for a turned-out ballet balance! Don't worry, falling is part of the fun!

LEAP

Ready to soar through the air? A leap is a jump from one foot to another. First, try jumping on two feet (that's called a SAUTÉ). Then try a small leap from one foot to the other, back and forth. Now you're ready to travel! Try a big run, kick out one leg and pretend you are leaping over a wide river to land on the other side! Extra points if you can keep your knees stretched straight as you leap in your GRAND JETÉ! Your arms, you say? Why, of course, please add some eagle wings to fly up as you leap!

STOMP

There's nothing more fun than being a stomping giant! Use your whole foot to stomp down hard like you are squashing a water balloon. Did you know that stomps and brushes are used in TAP dance to create RHYTHMS with your feet? Can you find a rhythm to stomp with your grownup? Maybe each of you can be a leader then a follower. Then try boom, boom, bah-dum, bing-boom! Make it strong and loud!

TIPTOE

Lighten up those feet as you rise higher! Let's RELEVÉ: lift to the balls of your feet. Then take a few tiny mouse steps in tiptoe. Can you do it forward, then sideways? Even backward??? For more fun, try playing some music as you tiptoe, then your grownup can surprise you by pausing the music so you can FREEZE like a statue until the music comes back on again.

We always love to end with a free dance! Move however you want to the music: fast, slow, high, low, sharp, smooth, get in the groove!

GREAT JOB, EVERYONE! KEEP ON MOVING AND USING YOUR IMAGINATION!

Photo: Christopher Baudesson

KERRY ALLAN is a dance educator and movement enthusiast! When she was little, she loved all things artsy: dance, music, drawing, writing, you name it. She combined her interests and now invites young movers to explore and imagine with her first book, *1 2 3, MOVE WITH ME!* Kerry currently lives in Maplewood, New Jersey with her family of groovers and movers.

To learn more, please visit kerryallanarts.com

TO ENJOY YOUR VIDEO OF 1 2 3, MOVE WITH ME

WITH ANIMATION AND AUDIO, VISIT:

OR SCAN HERE:

https://youtu.be/FJkxxm3bRvY

Milton Keynes UK
Ingram Content Group UK Ltd.
UKHW050222021224
451567UK00008B/70